IN THE CITY OF ROME

This is the city of Rome,

in which there is a…

gate.

This gate opens onto a street,

and the street leads to a...

plaza.

In the plaza there is a house,

and inside of the house, there is a...

hall.
From the hall, there is a flight of stairs.

The stairs go up to a…

door.
This door opens to a room.

In the room, there is a...

bed.
Next to the bed, there is a…
table.
Next to the table, there is a cage.

Inside the cage, there is a...

parrot.
This parrot manages to
get out of the cage,
that is on the table,

that is next to the…

bed,
that is inside the room,

that is behind the...

door,
that is at the top of the stairs,

that go down to the...

hall,
that is inside the house,

which is on the…

plaza,
that is on the street,

that leads to a…

gate,
which is in the city of Rome.